Google Wallet 2.0
© 2014 David W. Schropfer

Google Wallet 2.0

How Verizon, AT&T and Apple
effectively blocked Google, and how
a new technology from Austin Texas
will change Google's fortunes

By David W. Schropfer

Searching finance

Published under licence April 2014 by Searching Finance Ltd.

ISBN: 978-1-907720-89-5

About the author

David W. Schropfer is an international business leader with two decades of management experience ranging from telecommunications to payment systems. Mr. Schropfer is the CEO of Anchor ID, Inc. and was previously a Partner with the internationally recognized consulting firm, The Luciano Group, where he led its Mobile Payment and Mobile Commerce practice. Earlier in his career, he was Senior Vice President with IDT Telecom, and a Business Development Officer for Capital One. He has served on the Board of Directors for multiple companies, and is a frequent speaker at industry conferences and trade shows. After graduating Boston College, David earned an Executive MBA from the University of Miami.

About Searching Finance

Searching Finance Ltd is a dynamic new voice in knowledge provision for the financial services and related professional sectors. For more information, please visit www.searchingfinance.com

Table of contents

Table of figures

Abstract

It has been more than 2 1/2 years since the Google Wallet launched, and it is floundering. And no wonder; Google Wallet can function properly on a maximum of about 7% of the smartphones in the United States. Why is their addressable market only 7%? Google Wallet relies on a security technology that is owned by the mobile network operators, and only one of these operators (Sprint) has agreed to work with Google Wallet. Verizon, AT&T have simply blocked Google Wallet from their networks. To make matters worse, the communication technology that is also relied on by Google Wallet is being blocked by Apple on all iPhones. With enemies like Verizon, AT&T, and Apple, how can Google Wallet possibly succeed? The answer lies in a technology that was created only three years ago in Austin, Texas.

Executive Summary

What is happening at Google Wallet?

On April 14, 2014, the essential 'Tap and Pay' function in Google Wallet App stopped working on all smartphones that were not running its latest version of Android called 'Kit Kat'. On that day, Google Wallet deactivated many of its already scarce user population with no transition period. Why?

Why has it failed to capture our attention, and penetrate the marketplace after 2 1/2 years of effort and hundreds of millions of dollars of capital? Google has been indomitable in many areas of business that it has pursued, to date. But, Google Wallet it is failing to gain traction by any reasonable set of expectations. Why?

The answer is the story of a simple battle plan, where the Technology is the key to success, but the keepers of that technology have effectively blocked Google. And Amazon. And Facebook. And many, many others.

This report explores the Technology, Players, and the reasons behind the unusual evolution of the Mobile commerce industry. To understand mobile commerce, and the present defeat of Google, requires an understanding of several industries, and recognition of some new technology that has recently emerged.

The combination of new services, new technology, old industries, and new ideas engendered in the Google Wallet make the environment difficult to other entrants. Verizon and AT&T have come together in a mobile wallet product called Isis. AMEX and Visa have also announced products that appear to be similar to the Google Wallet. PayPal opened an actual retail location in New York City to demonstrate to merchants the shopping experience of consumers based on PayPal's product. Also, Amazon is rumored to be working on similar services as well. The Google Wallet, the Isis product, the Visa digital wallet – all share a common set of features and benefits to both retailer and consumer, despite the fact that none of these product have made it to the market or even a market test. All of these products have new business models that rely on a combination of revenue streams from different industries. An analysis of these revenue streams, and their potential, is critical to understanding these new products and the profit they will bring to the competitors.

The research and analysis presented in this report reaches one conclusion: if a lucrative market is blocked by the owners of a specific technology, then new technologies will emerge, and he market will flow freely.

Put another way, a free market economy will iron out the wrinkles, eventually. That is what is about to happen at Google Wallet.

Introduction to the Predicate Industries

If we don't understand where we have been, we can't understand where we are going. The technology and the market systems that have been developed over the last several decades– Half century really- have created trillions of case studies separating successful technologies from the failures; the successful market systems from the failures, and the successful business models from the failures.

This section explores the predicate industries of smartcards, mobile telecommunications, and a new industry called Trusted Service management (TSM). The payments industry and the mobile telecommunications industry became permanently ingrained in the smartcard industry back in the 1970s and 80s. But only now are these industries colliding to create new models and new ecosystems that have not experienced mass adoption. Google Wallet is currently in the middle of this collision, playing the role of the movable object and not the irresistible force. But that's about to change.

Smart Cards

The primary reason that Google Wallet is failing is due to Smart Card technology. To understand why, you must first understand what a smart card is, and why it works. If you are looking for a lesson on cryptography, you are in the wrong place. This section breaks down the basic functions of the smartcard and haw it is used for authentication and secure communication. Actual cryptography is significantly more complex than this section explains. But, Google Wallet was thwarted in its efforts to date because of this technology (and the companies that own it), so the layman's description is critical in understanding why that happened.

Smart card technology has been credited with solving significant end – user security problems in multiple industries. You're probably using a smartcard right now. They are used in corporate buildings to access secure areas, they're used in satellite dish receivers to make sure that you're paying for all the content you access, they're used in mobile phone devices to ensure that they are accurately and securely communicating on an authorized network, And they are presently changing the payments industry with the advent of what is commonly known as the chip and pin card.

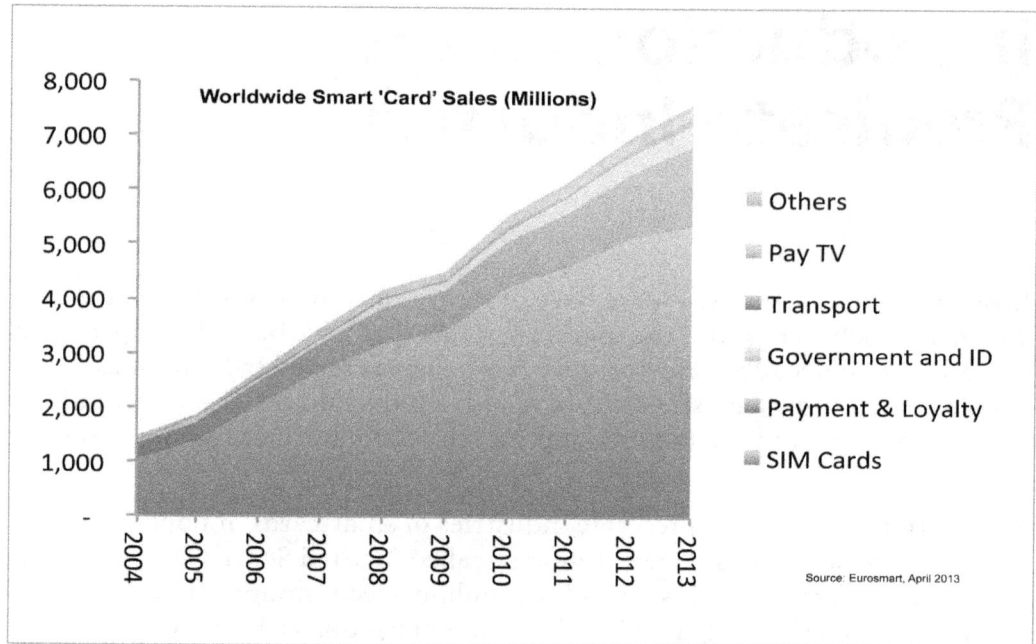

Figure 1: Worldwide Smartcard Sales

As the above figure shows, there was in excess of one smartcard sold for each man, woman and child on earth; and that was just for the year 2013.

Do we really need Smartcards in all of our products? Do we need to install them at a rate of more than the population of the world over and over again every year? From a strict market perspective, these product would not be selling at such an incredible rate if they did not work.

So how does a smartcard work, and what does it do? Any why has it unhinged Google Wallet?

Smartcard technology relies on a pair of computers. Any single computer cannot perform the function of a smartcard, at least as we are defining it here. The base idea behind the technology is that this pair of computers will share an identical secret code at any given moment in time.

Smart card technology relies on one central tenant: never transmit the "Secret code." At the moment that one of the computers needs to validate the other, a series of questions and answers is executed between the two machines. Have you heard of machine– 2 – machine (M2M) interfaces? Smartcard technology is an example of machine– 2 – machine.

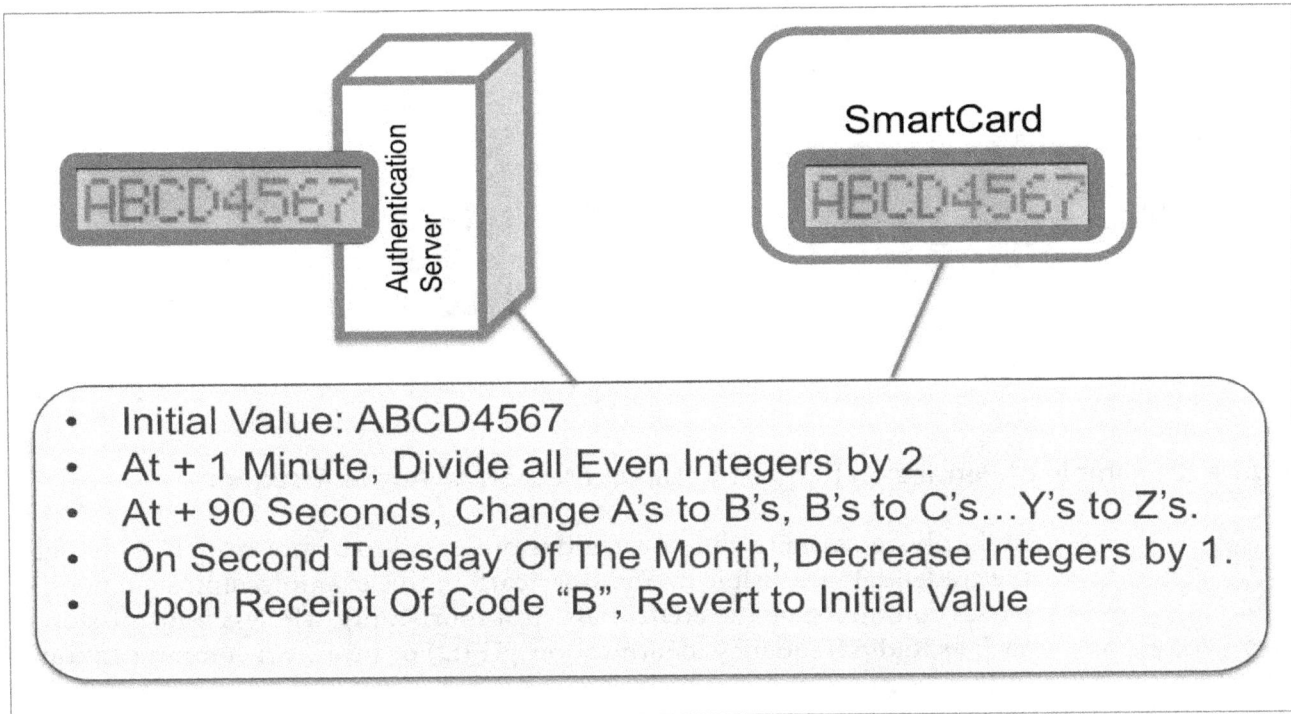

SmartCard

ABCD4567

Authentication Server

ABCD4567

- Initial Value: ABCD4567
- At + 1 Minute, Divide all Even Integers by 2.
- At + 90 Seconds, Change A's to B's, B's to C's…Y's to Z's.
- On Second Tuesday Of The Month, Decrease Integers by 1.
- Upon Receipt Of Code "B", Revert to Initial Value

Figure 2: Example of Initiation of a Smartcard

Note that the above figure is a crude example of what happens when a smartcard is activated. The cryptography around this process is infinitely more complex than this example, however the figure is useful in understanding the general process. Essentially, these two computers (the authentication server, and the smartcard itself) are programmed with an identical initial value, and a dynamic algorithm that continuously changes that value. Given that the value is constantly changing, it can be used as a proxy for any other number, such as an account number, a user identifier, or any other code. This example is being oversimplified because the audience for this paper is the financial industry, the investment community, and other interested parties. This is not a technical document.

Smart Card Authentication

The authentication of a smartcard can be accomplished in one of two ways: challenge question or direct. 'Direct' means that the smartcard simply shares the value of its secret code. For example, you swipe your card at a door-key reader to gain access to that door.

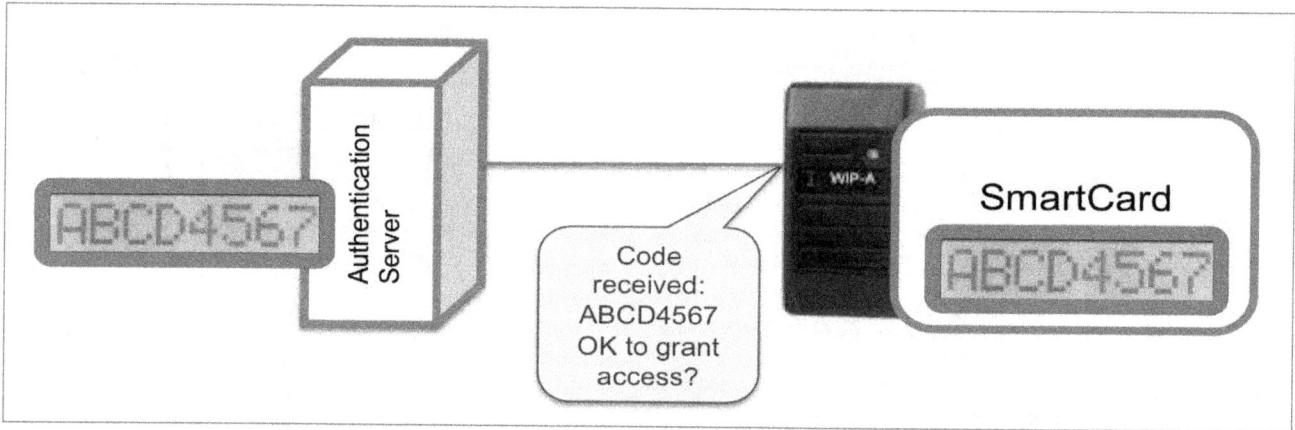

Figure 3: Example of Permission Request in Direct Method of Authentication.

In the above example, the smartcard is presented to a door reader. Although the credentials are visible on the smartcard in this example, almost all door passes communicate the credentials via a short-range wireless transmission such as Radio frequency identification (RFID) or near field communications (NFC).

The next step in the process of the smartcard authentication is performed by the authentication server. The role of the authentication server is to keep the credentials of each valid smartcard in lock-step with the card itself by running the same algorithm that is running on the card. In this way, the authentication server will be able to determine if the smartcard is valid at the moment it is presented. In the figure below, the authentication request from the card reader matches a current set of credentials on the authentication server, and access is granted.

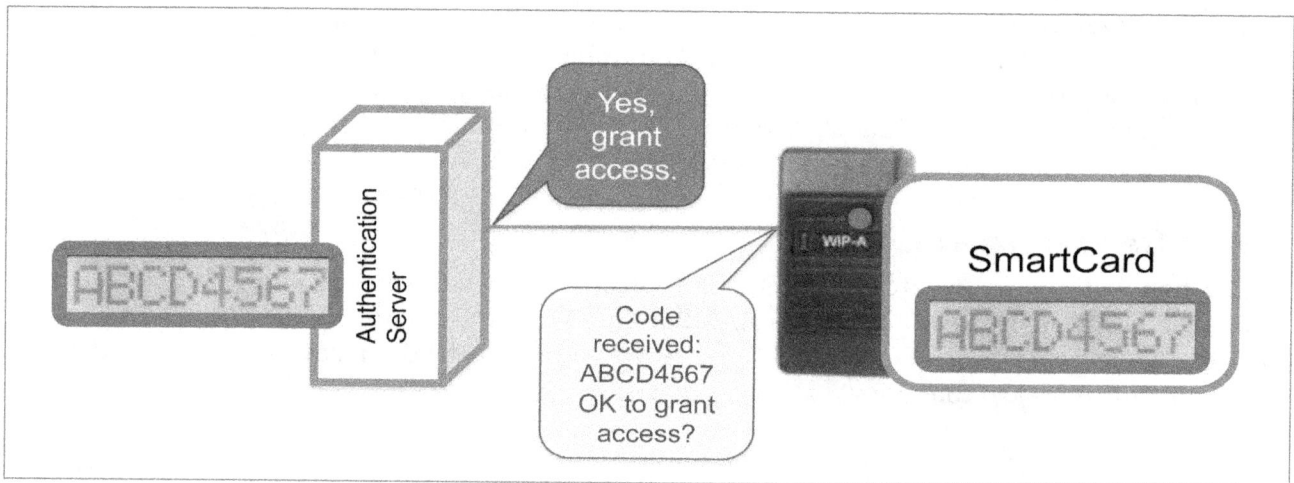

Figure 4: Example of Access Granted by Authentication Server

Note that, in the above example, a physical network interconnection exists between the door reader and the authentication server. But not all smartcard scenarios have access to a physical network, such as mobile phones, which rely on over-the-air communications.

The alternative method to authenticate smartcards with a server: poses a challeng question. The challenge question is a process that prevents the credentials from ever being transmitted between the smartcard and the server. (Again, this is a paper for businesspeople, not professional cryptographers.)

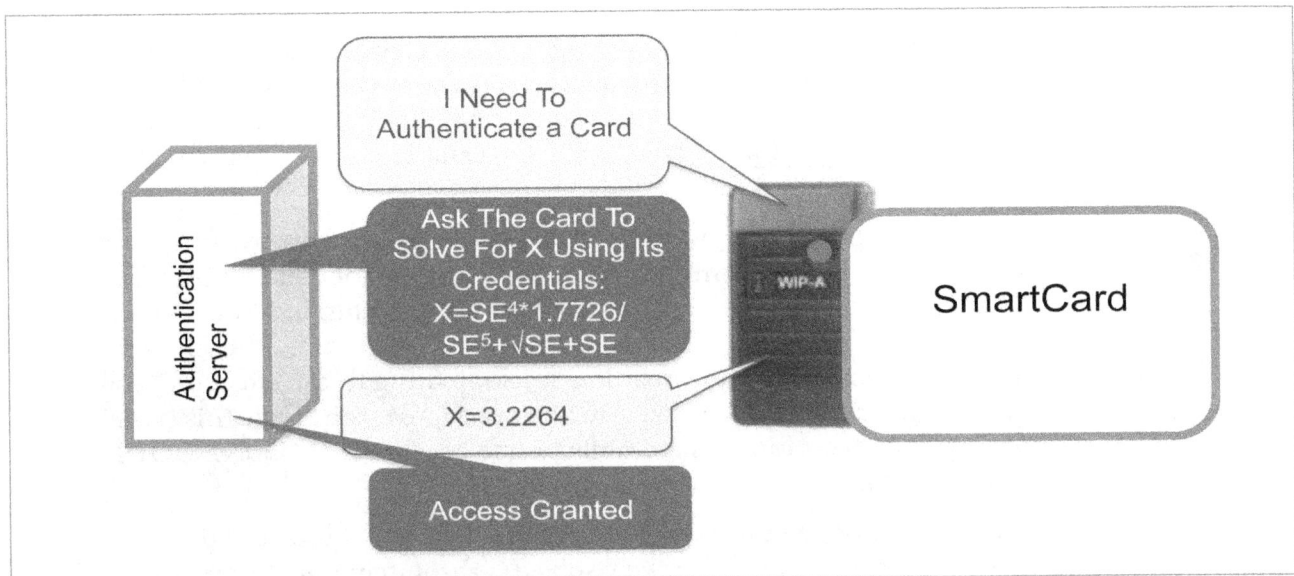

Figure 5: Example of Challenge Question Authentication

In this example, the only information transmitted between the server and the card reader is information about the credentials, but not the actual credentials. This is a significant additional security feature, as the mobile phone industry learned painfully in the USA in the 1980's.

Mobile Telecommunications

What happens when you turn on a mobile phone? The lights come on, and it is ready to use. Anything else? Yes; a machine-to-machine dialogue. Every time you turn on your phone, the mobile phone network has to do two things: determine if it recognizes its mobile network operator, and then prove to that network that it is an authentic phone that should be able to gain access to that network.

In the early mobile networks of the 1980's and early 1990's, the industry used a version of direct authentication, meaning that the mobile phones of that day transmitted an encrypted serial number to the network over the air. This method would prove to be a multi-billion dollar mistake.

Apparently, the fraudsters figured out a way to take the encrypted serial number of the mobile phone while it was being transmitted over the air. This led to two significant consequences, which could have been disastrous for the emerging mobile phone industry:

1. Cloning – The fraudsters learned to intercept the encrypted mobile serial number while it was being transmitted over the air, and then programmed that number into another device. This was called, 'Cloning.' The device that was reprogrammed by the fraudsters could make phone calls to anyone in the world, and the charges for those calls would appear on the victim's monthly invoice. And the cost of phone calls was significantly higher three decades ago.

2. Eavesdropping – If fraudulent phone charges was a big problem, the problem of eavesdropping was enormous. Another byproduct of a phone being cloned is that the phone reprogrammed by the fraudsters could listen to all conversations made on the victim's phone.

If you're not old enough to remember how crippling these security problems were, watch a movie from the 80's or early 90's. A good example is 'The Long Kiss Goodnight' with Gina Davis, or "Spy Games' starring Robert Redford and Brad Pitt which was released on 2001 but set in 1991. In each of these movies, a character can be heard to say something to the effect of, "You are on a mobile phone right now? Are you crazy? We can't have this (sensitive, or illegal) conversation on a mobile phone because SOMEONE COULD BE LISTENING."

Would the mobile industry have achieved it's present size and penetration if this problem was not definitively solved. Absolutely not. Something had to be done before tens of billions of dollars in infrastructure was lost. But, it was too late. Much of the billions invested in the initial infrastructure was simply lost, save the power supplies and physical infrastructure.

The solution that emerged – the solution you are using right now in the form of the cell phone in your pocket, is smart card technology. Here is how it worked (and still works today).

The first problem was separation. Given that the basic 'flip phone' was a functioning computer that, although it lacked an operating system, had the ability to perform basic functions like managing a contact list and even some primitive internet connectivity. The problem with any connected computer is that is could be corrupted by virus, malware, and other programs designed to work counter to the user's interests.

So – separate-but-equal was the solution. While this philosophy did not work out so well as a political mandate, it has become the industry standard for mobile devices. It works by creating a separate computer on the mobile phone, meaning that the processor is separate from the rest of the phone, the memory storage is separate, even the power supply is separate in most designs. Add the ability to connect with the rest of the mobile phone (or any other computer, but that will come later) and you have the opportunity for a highly secure environment. It was called the Subscriber Identification Module Card, better known as the SIM card.

The SIM card is a smartcard, which is the reason we spent an entire section on the definition and uses of the smartcard. Of you skipped that section, go back and read it. It is useful; here's why:

Operating as a smartcard, the SIM card uses the 'challenge question' method. Every time you turn 'on' your mobile device, it looks for a mobile network operator with which to connect. It may be in range of several mobile networks, but it can only connect with the one that programmed its smartcard.

Taking a step back, a SIM card is programmed when you buy your mobile phone. It is called an initiation – or activation -process, and it established the programming in your mobile phone on the day you purchased it.

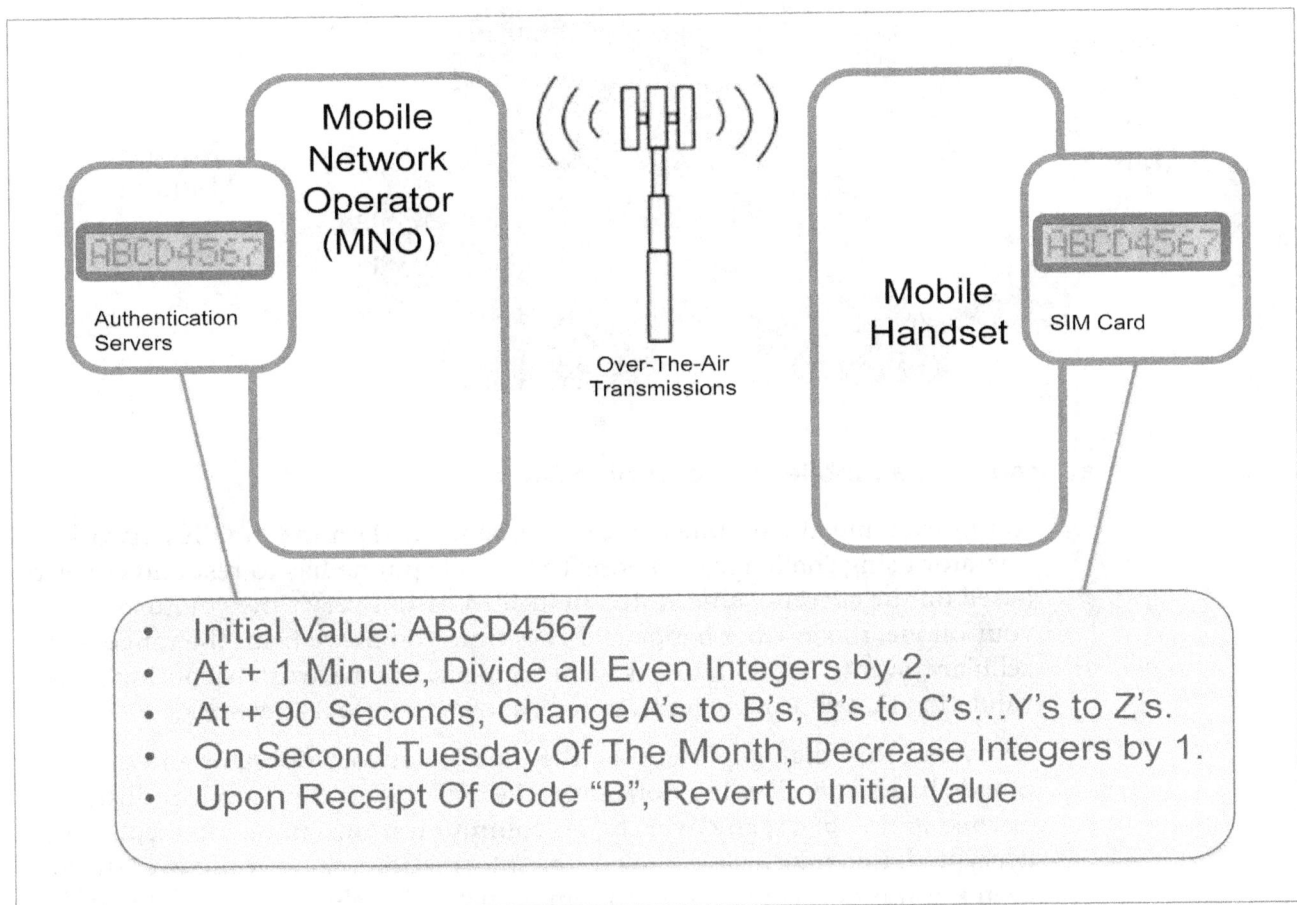

Figure 6: Initialization of a SIM Card in a Mobile Phone using the Secure Element

When you purchased the mobile phone that is currently in your pocket, this process occurred. As shown in the above figure, the smart card in your phone was programed with a Secret code (Or an "initial value") plus a series of commands to change that initial value. Does this diagram look familiar? It should. The programming of the SIM card is extremely similar to the programming of the smartcard as discussed in the previous section. Again – and I cannot overstate this– the cryptography involved with these events is remarkably more complex than I am describing here. But for the purpose of understanding the role of the smartcard in our common tech today, and understanding why Google Wallet is having such difficulty with this technology, this example explains exactly what you need to know. Simply stated: It's better then encryption. Here's why:

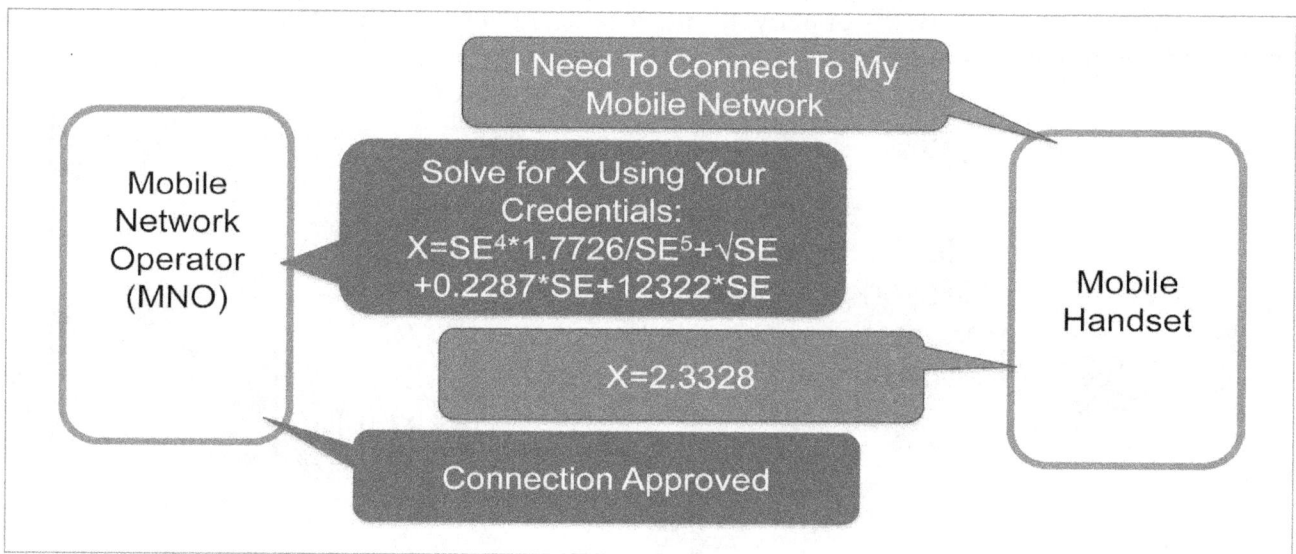

Figure 7: Authentication of a Mobile Phone Using a SIM Card

In this example, the mobile device is authenticated on the mobile network operator using challenge question. The mobile phone has to respond correctly based on the current value stored in its SIM card. Every time you turn on your phone, this is what happens. Every time you move from the range of one cellular tower to another, this is what happens. The network is continuously validating that your handset is, in fact, allowed to use its network.

Of course, this "dialogue" between the mobile network operator and the mobile handset is all being done over the air. And, as the mobile industry learned in the 1980's, any over the air communication can be intercepted and decrypted. But, take a close look at the information that is going over the air: even if it was decrypted it is both temporary and useless to a fraudster looking to exploit this information. For example, as described earlier in this section, the mobile phone would encrypt and transmit the same electronic serial number every time it attempted to authenticate itself on a network. But, as the above figure explains, smartcard technology ensures that the handset will transmit a different number (or alphanumeric combination) every time this process is repeated for two reasons: first, the network will never ask the same challenge question twice, which means the answer to the challenge question must always be different. Secondly, the answer to the challenge question is based on the value of the key at any given moment in time, and as explained earlier, this value is always changing. So, even if the network asked the same challenge question more than once to authenticate a mobile device (which it would not), again the answer transmitted from the air would never be the same twice because it is based on a value that is constantly changing.

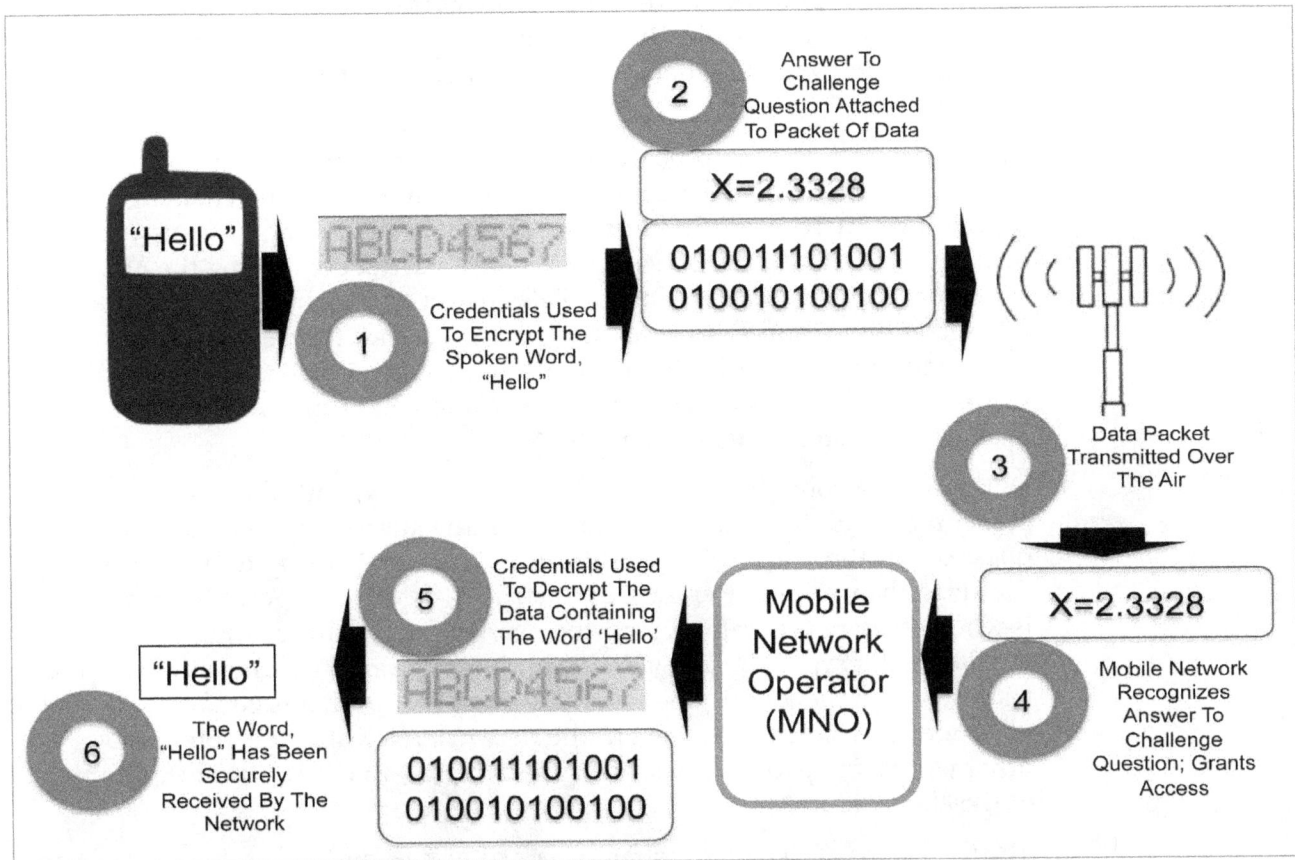

Figure 8: Multi-Factor Authentication in Voice and Text Data

The purpose of the above figure is to describe the remarkable security involved in simply communicating the spoken word hello from a mobile device onto a mobile network. This is a greatly simplified version of what is happening, but this general process ensures that nobody can listen to your phone calls.

Referencing the above figure, the first step (indicated by the number 1 inside of a red circle) is the digitization of a spoken word. As you probably know most voice communication is converted to a quantity of ones and zeros before it is sent over the air. This is a simplified definition of digital communications. Digital, of course, means ones and zeros are ultimately the form by which the voice communication travels. In contrast is Analog communication, in which the transmission– usually in the form of some sort of light wave, resembles the original audio signal. Digital communication bears no resemblance to the original audio signal, making it a little harder to intercept over the air.

What makes it even harder to decrypt these ones and zeros is the encryption key. As discussed in the previous section, the SIM card has a credential value that was used to answer the challenge question when the phone was turned on. This same credential is used in a second way–as an encryption key to effectively scramble the ones and zeros that were used to form the word 'hello'. Given that the network has the exact same credentials stored in its servers at any given moment in time, that will ultimately be used to decrypt these ones and zeros later when this data reaches the network in step five of the above figure.

In step two, the data is prepared for transmission over the air by the addition of the answer to the challenge question. Back in figure 7, the challenge question was used to authenticate the phone on a network. The answer to this challenge question is used to secure the data packet containing the ones and zeros that contain the word 'hello.' This answer to the challenge question will be used as an identifier, so when this packet reaches the network it will have the unique answer to a challenge question, which will tell the network that the packet is authorized to enter network, and which specific user has sent the package via their mobile phone.

With the data containing the word 'hello' encrypted with the current credentials, and the packet appended with the answer to the challenge question for the purpose of identification, the data is ready to be sent over the air to the network. Remember that the easiest access point for a fraudster is when the data is being transmitted over the air. In this example, however, the data is encrypted by a key that is both temporary and unavailable to the fraudster, and the identifying information of that packet is equally unavailable and indecipherable to anyone but the network for which it is intended. In other words, the packet travels over the air safely to the network in step three of the above figure.

The final steps of this process–Numbers four, five, and six in the above figure, The mobile network recognizes the answer to the challenge question, and routes the Data Packet to the appropriate decryption key. Once the key is applied in step five, the word 'hello' is decrypted, and is ready for secure transmission to the recipient via the mobile network.

So, this process– although it has been oversimplified in this example– is the reason that people cannot listen to your phone calls via mobile devices, and also why someone cannot make phone calls that are charged to your bill. These events almost never happen despite the billions of mobile phones currently in use around the world. In fact, most security you use regarding voice and text messaging have happened because the network itself was illegally or inappropriately accessed either by a corrupt employee, or other internal network breach. But, the over the air communication is as safe as present technology will allow.

Trusted Service Management (TSM)

Based on the success of the SIM card model in establishing a secure connection between a mobile device and a network, the Global System for Mobile communications Association (GSMA) came up with an idea called Trusted Service Management. Simply put, the GSM industry decided that they were successful in keeping one number secure on a mobile device (namely your mobile phone number), could they keep more than one number safe on the mobile device using the same method? The answer is, they could.

The mobile network operators quickly determined that managing other credentials on a mobile device was not their core business, and let the new TSM industry go to other players. However, only a handful of companies can competently access to SIM card without corrupting its original intent and purpose. So here's how it works:

> Definition of a Secure Element:
> A secure element (or "SE") is a highly-secure tamper-resistant system comprised of software and one of the three types of compatible hardware. It host confidential and proprietary code containing cryptographic 'keys (or data) following the rules set of the TSM industry, which was invented by the GSMA.
> The three types of hardware that are compatible with the SE are the Secure Identity Module (or SIM) Card, the embedded SE (embedded on the motherboard of the mobile device by the original equipment manufacturer),

Figure 9: Definition of Secure Element

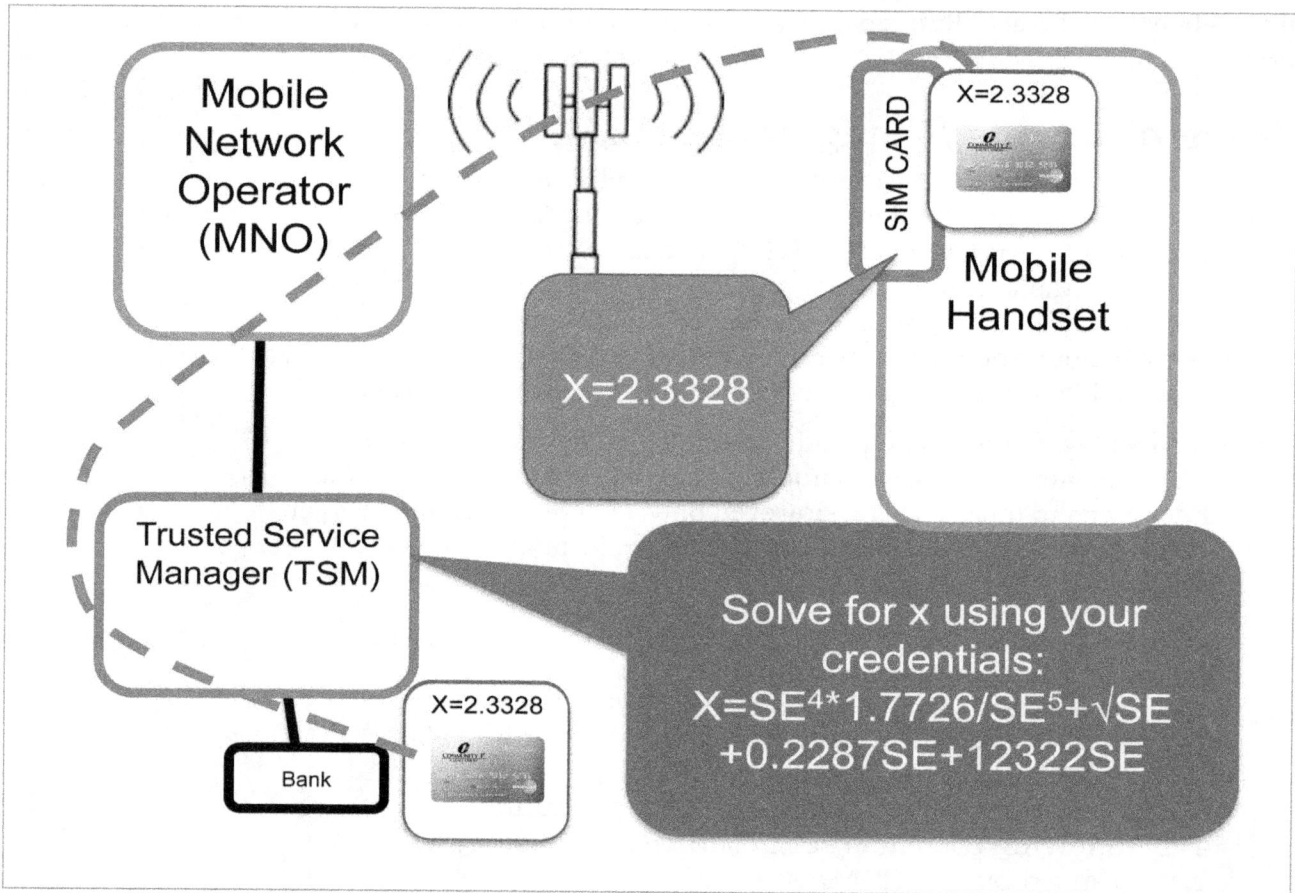

Figure 10: How a TSM Functions

In the above example, we see a bank that has contracted with a Trusted Service Manager. In this case, the function of the TSM is to take a set of credentials – in this case a credit card – and securely load these credentials on the mobile device.

As you can see in the above figure, the process of doing this is remarkably similar to the process of securing voice communication and basic authentication between the Mobile Network Operator and the mobile device. The bank starts by providing a token for the actual credit card number. This is important because the TSM never knows the actual 16 – digit credit card account number. Later in the process, however, the bank (and only the bank) will be able to associate the token with the actual 16 digit account number.

Of course, this system is limited to smartphones, not feature phones. Distinguishing characteristic between these two mobile devices is that feature phones have no operating system, and can only run simple Java applets, whereas smartphones have an operating system such as iOS or Android.

The first step in this process begins when the bank contracts with the TSM. The bank will also need to contract with the mobile network operator(s) to provide service to its clients. [As you will see in later chapters, this is exactly where Google Wallet failed because it successfully contracted with a TSM, but failed to contract with the mobile network operators.]

At the time these macro agreements are established between the bank, the TSM, and the mobile network operators, the TSM and the MNO's agree on a set of protocols that are programmed into a code set, which will be programmed in a form of Java. This Java code is then programmed into the bank's mobile app. So, when the user downloads the bank's mobile app, the mobile device grants permission for the bank's mobile app to write its proprietary Java code directly onto the SIM card. Note that the portion of memory within the SIM card that is used for this purpose is commonly referred to as the "Secure Element" as defined in Figure 9.

This is the "secret sauce" to the entire process. The SIM card is designed to be a completely separate computer within the mobile device or mobile phone. Typical apps, scripts, mobile websites, and other forms of computer code are absolutely denied access to the SIM card to prevent unauthorized reprogramming. So, only in this scenario as described in this section and the above figure can an application of any kind gain access to the SIM card. This is why the SIM Card is the most secure part of the mobile device.

TSM uses the same technology to secure a smart phone as a trusted device on networks other than your mobile network. In short, a TSM is responsible for ensuring the credentials of a particular service are stored properly on your mobile phone; after which the TSM uses the a network to communicate directly with the mobile phone to ensure the credentials have remained secure over time.

Given that the SIM card is the most secure part of the mobile device, the TSM uses the code running on the SIM card – or the portion of the SIM card commonly referred to as the Secure Element - to provision the banks credit card on the mobile device. The process starts with the typical challenge question, where the TSM challenges the phone to answer correctly based on the current value of the credential residing in the SIM card. If the mobile answers back correctly, then the card is ready for provisioning.

In figure 10, notice that the answer to the challenge question is exactly 2.3328. If you look closely at the figure, the credit card (depicted by the image of a MasterCard in a small red box) includes the answer to this challenge question within the data packet. This is called a "Header" of which the answer to the challenge question is one of many different values. These Header values determined the mobile device authorized to receive the packet, as well as the information needed by the mobile device to decrypt the token enclosed in the packet. In the above figure, the dotted line represents the bank sending the encrypted token through the TSM , over the air through the mobile network operator, and finally to the mobile device itself where it is decrypted and ready for use.

Technically, the TSM is not one entity but two. As described earlier, the Mobile Network Operators have no interest in managing credentials other than their 10 digit mobile phone numbers. Therefore, they contracted with a TSM of their choice, called a "root" TSM. The Root TSM and each Mobile Network Operator share extremely confidential information between them, namely: the Mobile Network Operator's secret code which allows permission for an application or firmware running on the mobile device to access the SIM card. Protecting this code is extremely important to the Mobile Network Operator's business model because – as described in the previous section – this code protects the SIM card from being accessed by any other software, malicious or otherwise. Given that the SIM card was largely responsible for creating consumer confidence around the security of mobile devices, the proprietary code to access the SIM card was shared only to a vendor of the mobile network operator. So in this case, the mobile network operator hires a Root TSM as a vendor to perform this function.

If the mobile network operator hires a root TSM, then the service provided to a bank (or a company like Google Wallet) is called a "Service Provider TSM" or SP – TSM. The job of the SP TSM is to manage the credentials between the client (again, a bank or Google Wallet or other such company) and the root TSM. The job of the root TSM is to get those credentials onto the SIM card on the mobile device with the permission of the mobile network operators.

… with the permission of the mobile network operators. This is where the concept went wrong for Google.

How the Mobile Operators challenged Google

Like most companies, Google Wallet has identified the smartcard system behind TSM as the best and obvious winner in the security standard of the upcoming Mobile Wallet Industry. The problem is, the mobile network operators actually own the SIM card in your phone, which makes them the gate keeper to this powerful smartcard technology.

Google, of course had no trouble hiring an SP TSM. It chose the payment processor which touches roughly 2 out of every 3 payment card transactions in the United States every year: First Data.

The TSM industry was young on September 19, 2011 when Google Wallet was originally launched, so it was a new business line for First Data. First Data, wisely choosing not to invest in the buildout of the new SP TSM operational infrastructure, chose to contract through a company called CorFire. See figure below:

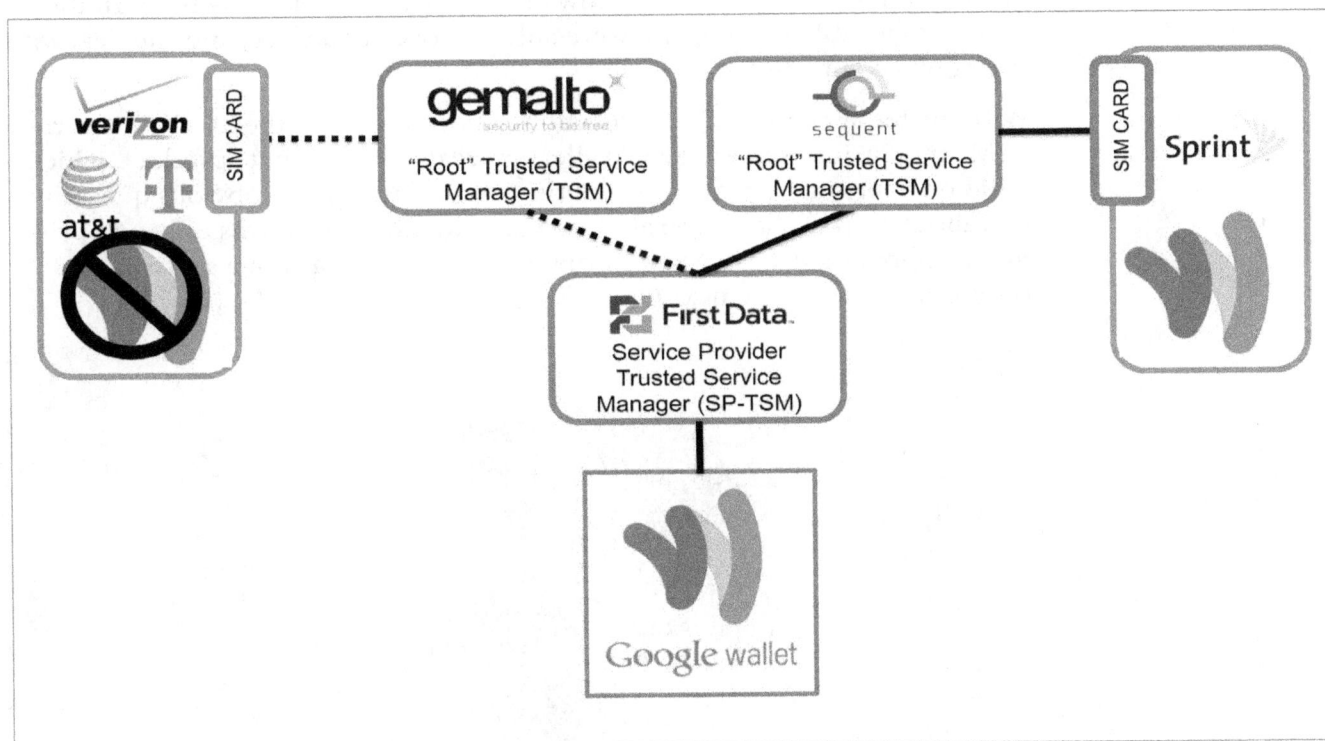

Figure 11: Mobile Network Operators and TSMs Involved in Google Wallet 1.0 and 1.5

In the above figure, the boxes outlined with a red line indicate that the system worked properly.

In the center of the figure, we see that Google Wallet contracted with First Data to do all of the SP TSM services. As described in an earlier section of this report, the job of an SP TSM is to manage the credentials between the client (Google Wallet) and the root TSM. In this case, the root TSM for Sprint is a company in California called Sequent. Sequent was able to manage the handshake between the SIM card on a mobile phone, and First Data.

Before the Google Wallet would work on Sprint phones, Google Wallet needed one more relationship: a relationship directly with Sprint. For the secure element system to work properly, a small amount of memory on the SIM card must be used to store the TSM's code. Because the SIM card is property of the mobile network operator, only the mobile network operator can "rent" space on the SIM card to third parties for this purpose. This is exactly what happened between Google Wallet and Sprint; Google negotiated a rate by which it would be allowed to install the TSM code directly onto the SIM card, and in exchange, Google paid 'rent' for the kilobits it used on the SIM card.

The TSM code takes extremely small amounts of memory, roughly 3 or 4 kb, but the mobile network operator is the only entity that can rent this space, making it the "supply" relatively low and the demand relatively high. In the end, Google Wallet and Sprint were able to work out a price, and the deal with Sprint was completed.

With the fee agreements in place, and the contracts with the SP TSM, the root TSM, and Sprint itself, Google Wallet was ready to launch its product, which it did on September 19, 2011. At the time of the launch, the obvious question was about market share. The ability to use Google while it was only on Sprint mobile phones locked out 83% of the market, which was not a sustainable position, as seen in the next figure.

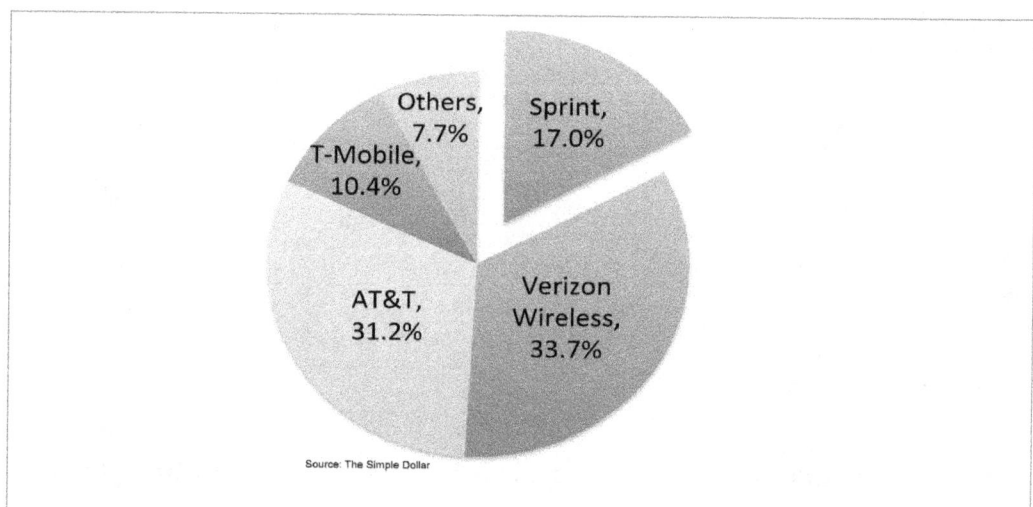

Source: The Simple Dollar

Figure 12: Market Share on Google Wallet 1.0 and 1.5 Mobile Operator Penetration

The management of the token between Google Wallet and (ultimately) the secure element on the SIM cards of Sprint mobile customers functioned properly. But that was not enough from a market share perspective. But the above figure shows that only 17% of mobile handset users in the United States were able to use the Google Wallet product, which is another way of saying that 83% of all public advertising would essentially be wasted until Google Wallet began working on the mobile phones of other networks. In a subsequent chapter, we will see Google Wallet's addressable market drop from 17% to about 7% because Apple blocked Google Wallet from the iPhone also, although Sprint only began selling the iPhone about one month after the launch of Google Wallet; iPhone penetration to Sprint users is currently between 35% and 40%.

Obviously, Google intended to expand its service to the networks of Verizon, AT&T, and others. Google assumed with its deep pockets, demonstrated willingness to pay to rent kilobits on a SIM card, and a strong existing relationship with the mobile network operators via its Android operating system, it would be able to negotiate similar contracts with Verizon, AT&T, and T-Mobile. Google Wallet was making a logical assumption because its Android system was enjoying market share of more than half of all phones shipped worldwide every year (in the year 2013, that figure increased to over 70% worldwide), making it the most prolific smartphone operating system by far.

So why didn't Google Wallet successfully reach an agreement with AT&T, Verizon wireless, or T-Mobile? It was not a technical problem. As seen in Figure 11: *Mobile Network Operators and TSMs Involved in Google Wallet 1.0 and 1.5*, First Data was able to work with the root TSM of these three carriers, a company called Gemalto. Given that Google Wallet was able to successfully negotiate an agreement to "rent" a few kilobits of space on the secure elements of Sprint phones, it should have been able to reach the same agreement with the other carriers. But Google Wallet failed to negotiate that same simple agreement with Verizon wireless and AT&T after trying for almost three years. What was the motivation behind Verizon wireless and AT&T? In a word, it was a new company called: Isis.

What is ISIS?

Isis (www.paywithisis.com) is a joint venture between AT&T, Verizon Wireless and T-Mobile. Isis is a mobile wallet product designed to provide the same services and payment options as other major mobile wallets. Its main competitor is – you guessed it – Google Wallet.

Isis was announced in a press conference on November 16, 2010. At that time, Isis was projecting to be a new mobile wallet, but it also was endeavoring to create a new payment scheme to compete with MasterCard, Visa, and American Express. Its CEO, Michael Abbott, convinced Isis's steering committee (representatives from each of the three joint-venture partners) that consumer adoption was critical, and convincing customers to both pay with a different form factor (the mobile device) and pay with a different type of payment (i.e. Isis card the as opposed to a Visa card or MasterCard) would significantly impede consumer adoption. So, on July 19, 2011 – a mere eight months after its initial announcement – Isis changed its business plan and announced a partnership with Visa, MasterCard, and American Express. Isis previously partnered with Discover card at the time of the announcement.

The Isis platform was built by C-Sam (which was acquired by MasterCard in February 2014) and is designed to be a closed network. For example, only the Isis platform can access credentials and data in the system.

Notice that Sprint is not part of this joint venture. This decision is consistent with Sprint's market position; Sprint is pursuing an 'open' format which will allow multiple parties and competitors to do business directly with Sprint for the purpose of accessing the secure element, providing wallet services to Sprint customers, and other products and services that require a smart phone for delivery.

Apple blocks Google, Isis, and Everyone

Like it or not, Apple is incredibly smart. It found a way to keep all mobile wallets off of its iPhones, which is why neither Isis nor Google Wallet can function without clumsy external devices on any iPhone. Here's how Apple is accomplishing this:

1. RADIO REQUIRED: to present a card, or any payment type, or most loyalty cards in the fastest easiest way possible, the phone needs to communicate directly with the retail cash register, also known as a Point-Of-Sale (POS) device. See figure, below.

NFC Chip

Figure 13: Diagram Of Isis Mobile Wallet Presented For Payment At POS

2. RADIOs EXIST: NFC & BLE: A mobile phone cannot plug in to a POS device using a wire or any other kind of physical connector. Therefore, it needs a radio signal. The radio signal that seems to have the most support is called Near Field Communication (NFC), which acts as a very short-range two-way radio. Bluetooth is another example of a short range radio that can link two computers, however, unlike NFC, Bluetooth spends a lot of the mobile devices energy while waiting for another computer with which to connect – which

drains the battery unnecessarily. This was resolved in late 2013 with a new invention called Bluetooth Low Energy (BLE), which stays dormant until it is 'woken up' by an authorized system. Apple launched a product called iBeacon in 2013, which may indicate that Apple will use BLE instead of NFC. Either way, these radios create access to the mobile device, and access needs to be secured to keep out the fraudsters and thieves.

3. RADIOS CREATE SERIOUS VULERABILITIES: The problem with the NFC chip is that it does not require paring or network acceptance by the user. If it is within range on another NFC Chip, it connects without asking the user. The limiting factor is the range – NFC chips need to be within 4 inches of each other to function properly. So, the good news if that if a thief or a fraudster wanted to use the NFC chip to gain malicious access to a mobile phone, they would have to be within 4 inches of the victim's device. But that is not good enough in the world of very clever fraudsters, because there are a variety of ways that a malicious device can be within 4 inches of a victim device without the victim ever knowing it, such as a crowded subway platform, a seat in a crowded movie theater, and many, many other scenarios. To solve this, the NFC chip had to be linked to something that could provide a significantly better level of security than we're used to seeing on a mobile device. The secure element was the perfect solution.

4. NFC LINKED TO SECURE ELEMENT: In almost all commercial deployments of NFC chips and mobile devices, the chip itself is installed in this SIM card, or in some cases built into the phone in a way that can only be accessed by the SIM card. In other words, for the NFC chip to function at all, it needs to get permission from the SIM card, and the secure element operating on the SIM card. So, if a thief was trying to access your mobile phone via NFC by sitting next to you in a crowded movie theater, the thief's program would not have the secure credentials stored in the secure element of your phone, and therefore the NFC attack simply would fail. The secure element became the universal safeguard against unauthorized access through the NFC chip.

5. APPLE AVOIDS BUILDING NFC INTO MOBILE DEVICES, BLOCKING ISIS and GOOGLE WALLET: In a strategic move, Apple simply chose not to add the NFC chip to any model iPhone, or any of the SIM cards it uses within any of the iPhone's. Technically, the SIM cards used by iPhones could be used to allow the mobile network operator and its root TSM to install a few lines of code within the memory of the SIM card, but none have done so because it would be useless without an NFC chip.

Apple has a second method of defense worth mentioning, which is: Apple approves all applications available on the App Store. To upload the code into a SIM card, an app would need to be downloaded from the Apple App Store, and installed on the iPhone. Apple could simply reject any application that attempted to do that, although such rejection has not been made public knowledge so we don't know if that is happened yet. Regardless, Apple's strategy of intentionally designing all iPhones without NFC, and intentionally choosing SIM cards that explicitly exclude an NFC chip, has effectively blocked NFC – based mobile wallets (including Isis and Google Wallet).

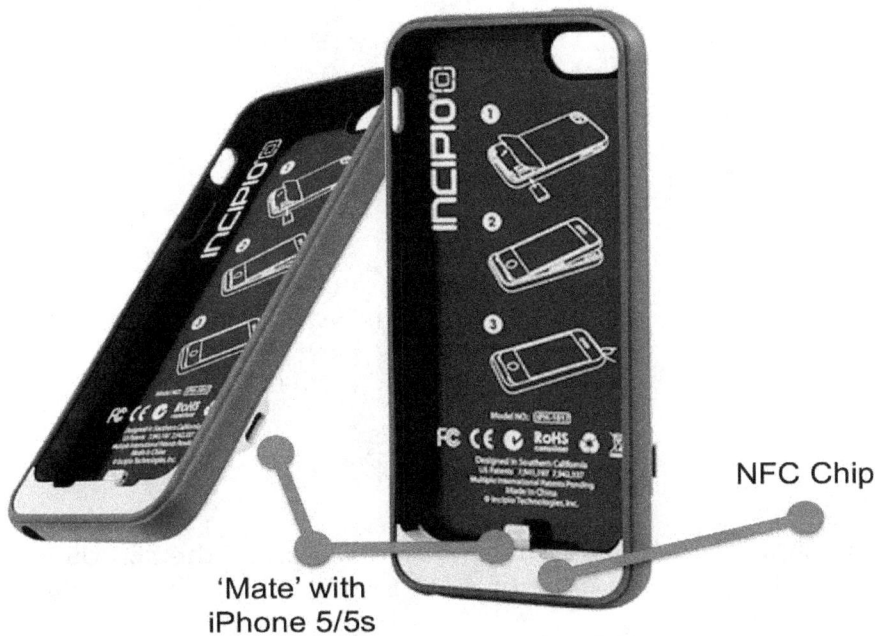

Figure 14: Diagram of Isis NFC case for iPhone 5S

In the above figure, we can see the Isis attempts to add an NFC chip to the iPhone 5 and 5S. Notice that there is a "mate" connector within the case. This allows the case to connect via the access port on the bottom of the iPhone, which the case uses for both power, and access to the rest of the iPhone, including the secure element in the SIM card. But, if the case uses the port on the iPhone, the case also needs to provide a duplicate of that port so that the user can plug in a typical power cord, sync cord or other products that require the use of this port.

While the solution is functional, it is far from elegant. It is also costly; this simple black case costs $69. Other similar cases retail for as much as $129. That's a very high price to pay to include an NFC chip – which costs about three dollars – into an iPhone. While exact figures are not known on how many users are adopting this technology, all those users would need to choose to buy a case like the one depicted in the figure, above to use the Isis wallet. And, iPhone users are still unable to use the Google Wallet at all, even with such a case, because Google is being blocked by the three Isis mobile network operators.   Google has launched an app for the iPhone, but it is not a fully functional product, as we will see in the next section.

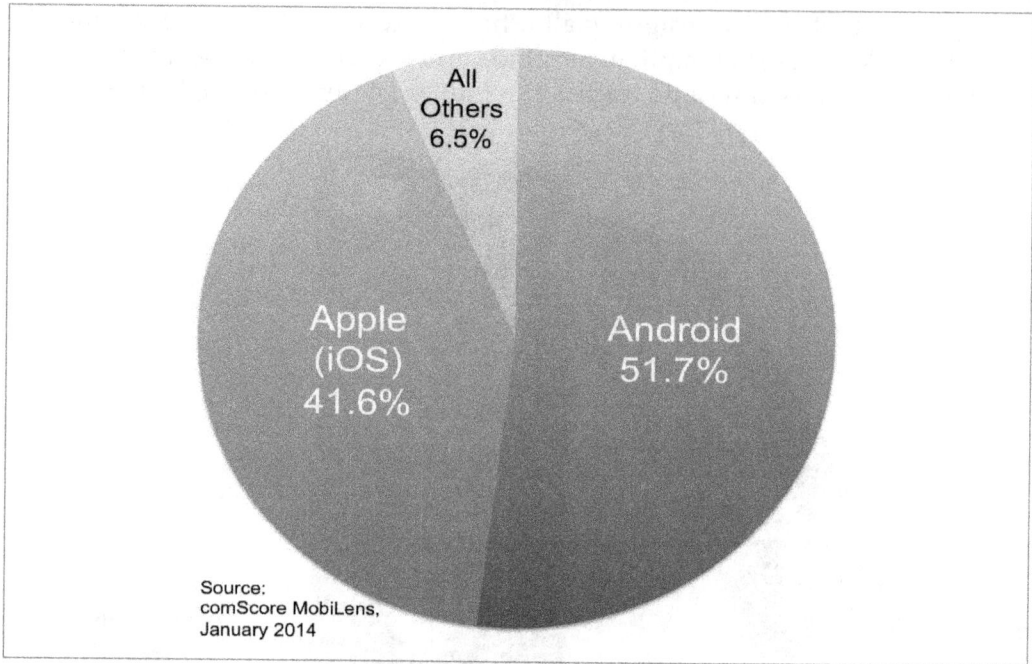

Figure 15: Apple iOS Market Share vs Android and Others in US, January 2014

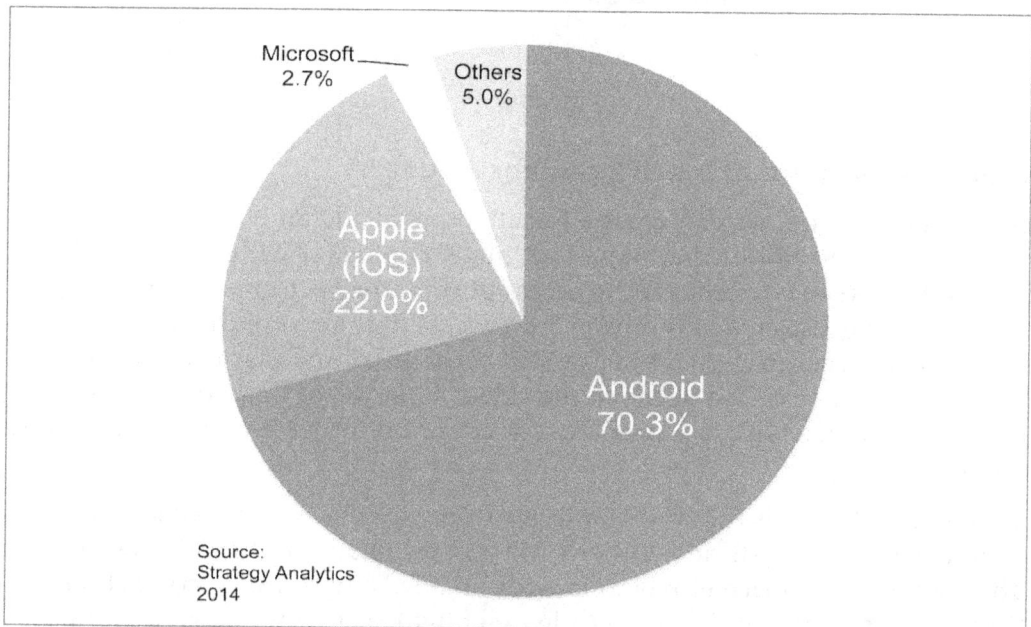

Figure 16: Worldwide Apple iOS Market Share vs Android and others, Calendar Year 2013

As the above two figures describe, Apple enjoys a significant share of the smartphone market in the United States, and the world. In 2013, roughly 42% of all smartphones shipped in the United States were Apple iPhones. Again, only 17% of United States users are Sprint customers, which means Google Wallet users are limited to that 17%. Now consider that less than half of that 17% uses an iPhone, and Google Wallets available market share falls to about 7% or less. It is difficult; very difficult, to effectively penetrate a market where your maximum market share is only 7%.

Worldwide, however, as the above figure shows, AppleShare slips to a mere 22%. But, that is not good news for Google Wallet because Google Wallet is not available as an app outside the United States.

How Google is Combating the Problems?

Google had to come up with a way to generate users and market share given the incredibly hostile environment of the emerging mobile wallet industry. Here are some of the tactics it used (or is presently using):

Cloud-based payments

The one product that Isis offers that Google is no longer pursuing is local card presentment (although Citi cards and some other cards still work in this way, but this is leftover technology from Google versions 1 and 1.5; Google is not adding more banks to its roster for this purpose). Local card presentment is the ability to actually present a card directly from the mobile phone to a payment device. Google Wallet's replacement solution to this is known as a "cloud-based" payment, meaning that all the credit cards are stored in the cloud on a secure Google server, therefore no actual credit card information is stored on the user's mobile phone (except in cases of the Citi card and other legacy cards from earlier version of Google Wallet). So how does Google Wallet "present" a credit card to the merchant if all the credit cards are stored in the cloud? Google simply creates an alternate MasterCard account for each user.

The alternate MasterCard contains the only credentials used directly on the mobile phone. It is a 16 digit number that the user doesn't know. In most cases, the user doesn't even know that the MasterCard exists at all. This MasterCard is essentially Google's account, and the merchant charges Google when this card is presented through the Google Wallet. Google wants to get paid by the user, of course, so Google charges the user's credit card for the amount of the transaction. Put another way, Google pays the merchant with Google's credit card, and then Google charges the User's real credit card to get reimbursed. Sound efficient? It's not. But it solves a functional problem for Google, and it allows Google to operate in the market while it irons out the inefficiencies that exist in its workflow.

Physical card

Yes, the Google Mobile Wallet has a physical plastic credit card. See the figure below. On the reverse side of this card is the 16-digit alternate Mastercard number that Google creates for each user. It works anywhere Mastercard accepts a magnetic stripe, but the physical card confounds the underlying conveniences provided by a digital wallet.

Figure 17: Photo of Physical Google Wallet Credit Card

P2P payments

The one product that Google Wallet has which Isis does not have his peer-to-peer (P2P) payments; the ability to send and receive money between non-merchants. Anyone with a Gmail account can send and receive funds through Google Wallet. Although Isis does not primarily support P2P payments, it uses American Express Serve card, which can facilitate peer-to-peer payments. Google, however, manages peer-to-peer payments through its proprietary system.

Apple App – no payments

The Google Wallet app for the iPhone should be called something other than a 'Wallet', primary because it does not support payments. That's right – a wallet that you can't use to pay. It is logical to assume that Google simply wanted to be able to add an 'Apple App Store' download button to its website, because the app itself does almost nothing, as we see in the figure below. Note that this app is limited only to a handful of functions, none of which are POS payments. They are: "Send Money' (Peer to Peer Payments), Transactions (completed online or on another device), 'Wallet Balance,' 'Offers' (coupons and discounts) and 'Loyalty' (retail loyalty programs).

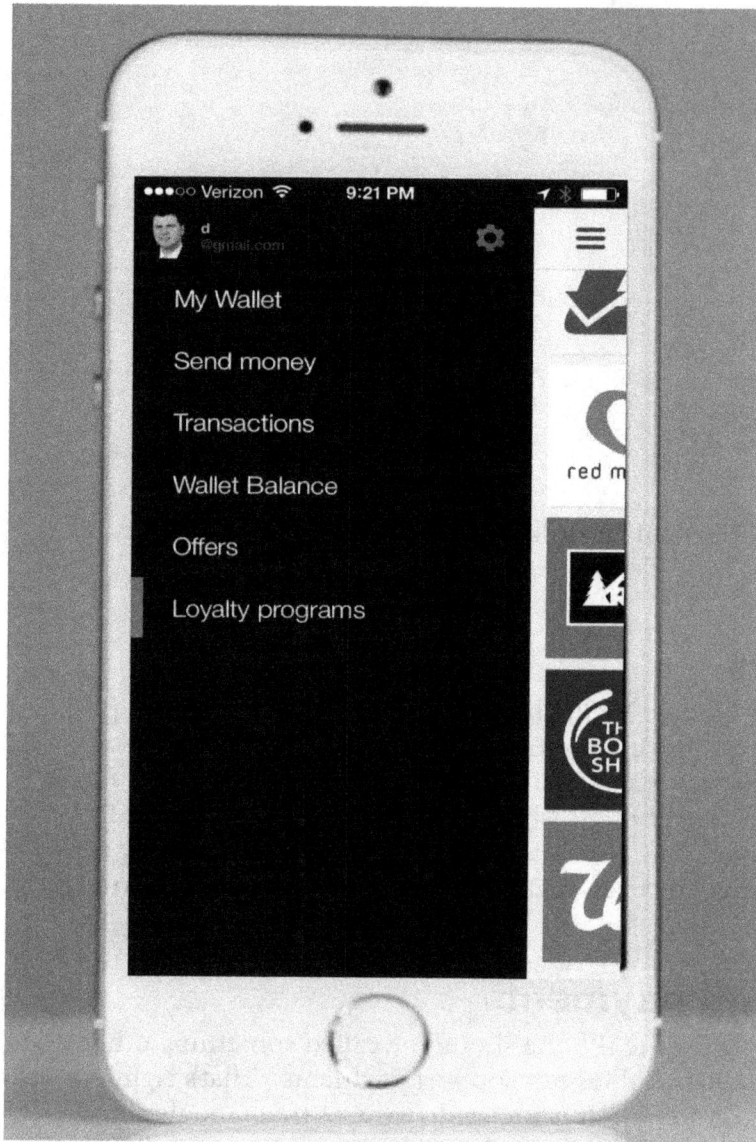

Figure 18: Diagram of Actual Menu on the Google Wallet App on Apple's iPhone 5S

Common items between Google Wallet and Isis

The Isis mobile wallet shares two significant features with the Google Wallet. Namely:

- reloadable stored value card – meaning that the product can be reloaded with other credit cards. Isis uses the American Express 'Serve' product which can accept cash-reloads at tens of thousands of retail locations nationwide, as seen in the figure below. Google Wallet's prepaid card can only be reloaded with other credit cards.

FREE Cash Reloads at the Register

At over 15,000 CVS/pharmacy® stores & participating 7-ELEVEN® locations

Add cash for FREE at over 15,000 CVS/pharmacy® and participating 7-ELEVEN® locations. Just give your cash and your American Express Serve® Card to the cashier and your money is immediately added to your Card.

Visit **serve.com/addcash** to find cash loading locations in your area.

serve® Your Full Service Reloadable Prepaid Account

08-03659-010

Figure 19: Sample of Mail Insert sent to AmEX's Serve Customers in January, 2014

- loyalty and marketing products – Google Wallet in its first 2.5 years has managed to attract a shockingly small list of loyalty partners. Available on the Google Wallet as of January 2014 were only fifteen different companies. Of these, 40% were in the travel industry, as we see in the figure below:

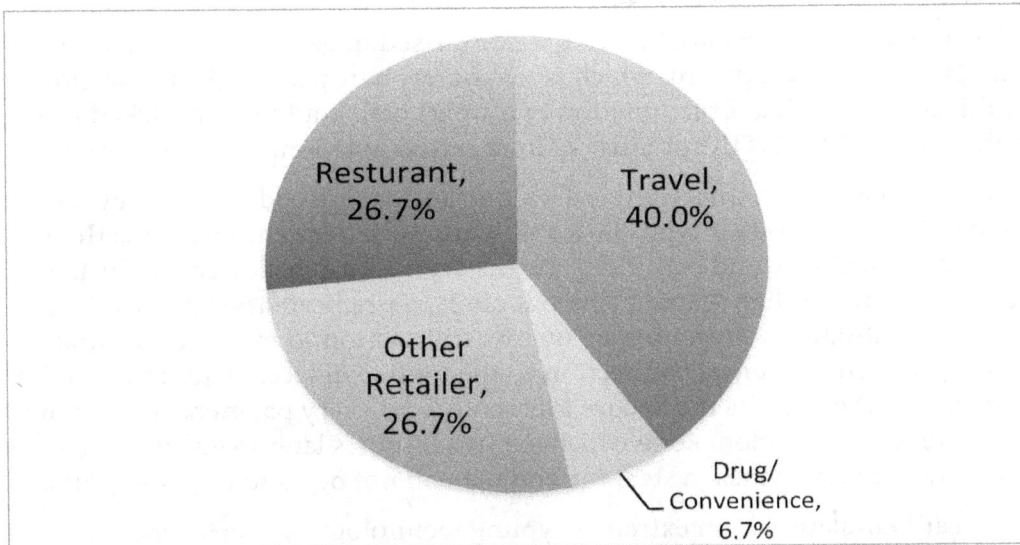

Figure 20: Distribution of Google Wallet Loyalty Programs by Industry

Host Card Emulation saves Google Wallet?

Is Google Wallet Finished? Hardly.

Google has replaced senior executive that chased the wrong solution for too long, consolidated Google Checkout and Google Wallet into one product, added peer-to-peer (P2P) payments, entered the iPhone (albeit with a stripped-down version). These are important measures, but none are capable of truly making Google Wallet accessible to the vast majority of the marketplace.

But, Google's Android 4.4 Operating System adopted a new technology called Host Card Emulation just days before this report went to press. Google Wallet is likely to adopt it, too.

What is Host Card Emulation?

All smartcards rely on hardware. As we discussed in earlier chapters, the SIM card is a form of smart card, which is, of course, hardware in the possession of the user. But, what if the function of a smart card could be mimicked using only software? That is the premise of host card emulation.

The main output of a smartcard is a unique and secure code (a.k.a. 'key' or 'credential'). This code is typically an alphanumeric sequence which is then used to authenticate and communicate between a mobile device and its host servers (see the earlier chapter, "introduction to predicate industries"). Host Card Emulation, however, uses a payment transaction to push a credential through a secure Internet connection to the mobile device. After that, the code works the same as the Secure Element. And every payment transaction generates a new, random code which expires minutes later to ensure that even if the fraudster manages to steal the code, it will not be valid for a long time.

Host card emulation is an extremely young technology. It was invented in 2011 by he founders of SimplyTapp, Doug Yeager and Ted Fifelski in Austin, Texas. The first commercial release was only a year later on August 29, 2012. But the biggest endorsement came in November 2013 when Google released Host Card Emulation integrated with its new Android 4.4 operating system release called Kit Kat. Then, in February 2014, Host Card Emulation won another substantial victory when Visa and MasterCard declared their support for Host Card Emulation for payment processing.

Why does this matter to Google Wallet? As discussed earlier, the NFC chip requires a high level of security because of it's easy access, so it is often linked solely to the secure element in the SIM card of the device. With host card emulation, however, the product of the SIM card –the secure code – can be used to give the NFC chip what it needs to turn on and function. With this technology, the Google Wallet, or any app running on Android 4.4 with the US SIM card, can access the NFC chip.

This is the game changer.

Any app, including Google Wallet running on Android 4.4 with the US SIM card – Regardless of Which Carriers is Being Used – can access the NFC chip which is critical for Google Wallets point-of-sale functionality. That means that Google can finally function properly on Verizon, AT&T, and T-Mobile,

As of the writing of this paper, Google Wallet has not yet updated its app to use Host Card Emulation, nor had any other apps been released on Android using this technology. That will change quickly. We can comfortably predicted that when Google Wallet is released using host card emulation, it will be available to all users of Android phones running on Android 4.4, whether that user is on the Verizon wireless network, the AT&T network, the T-Mobile network, or the Sprint network. Note that Host card emulation does not immediately solve the iPhone problem for Google Wallet, but there is a reasonable expectation that Host Card Emulation will soon tackle that problem also for Google Wallet.

Summary and Conclusion

Mobile wallets work because they add value to the consumer. Everything else is redundant.

If mobile wallets didn't make the consumer's life easier, or provide convenience where it didn't exist before, mobile wallets would not work. But they do work.

Think about your physical wallet in your pocket right now. You probably have credit cards, some loyalty cards, and some identification cards. Maybe even a few coupons for discounts at your local store. The problem is, your leather wallet doesn't tell you what you have, or don't have, at any given moment. It doesn't communicate between your loyalty cards in your Visa card, between your coupon and your debit card, or between any of the other products you are carrying now in your physical wallet.

Your physical wallet does not think. Your mobile wallet does. That's the difference, and that's why mobile wallets, in time, will succeed.

Google Wallet is clearly capable of being a front runner, although there really are no front runners for the nascent industry of mobile wallets because adoption is presently so low. Google Wallet may or may not have the marketing messaging, product design, or commitment to convince tens of millions of users to adopt their mobile wallet product. That problem remains to be solved.

The problem that seems to have been solved is that of addressable market. As of February 2014, the full Google while the product is only available in the United States on the Sprint mobile network (17% of the US mobile market) and on less than half of Sprint users that use an iPhone, which leaves a scant 7% of the US mobile market as Google Wallet's addressable market. When Google Wallet integrates Host Card Emulation, it could access more than 50% of the US Mobile market within the time it takes Android users to upgrade from their existing version of Android to Android 4.4 (KitKat).

The iPhone could be a problem for Google Wallet until Apple decides to include NFC in its phones. But the possibility exists that a combination of Bluetooth low energy (BLE) and host card emulation could give Google Wallet a way to communicate from an iPhone app directly to a point-of-sale device.

Google Wallet, Isis, and other mobile wallets have a long way to go before they earn consumer trust and confidence. But the basis of their business model is sound because it adds convenience to the user experience. The technology is sound because it is based on smart cards, which have trillions of use-cases proving their efficacy. Host card emulation is young, and unproven in the mass-market at present. But, if it is proven to be better then any other form of encryption, which is possible, then it will quickly change the availability of these wallet products in the marketplace, and Google Wallet stands a fighting chance of gaining the market-dominating position it seeks.